No better liner was ever fitted to any racing car

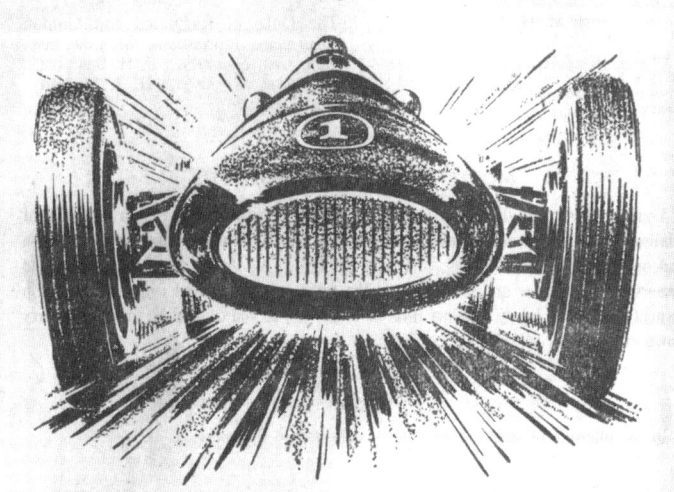

When high performance counts you can rely on

MINTEX
BRAKE LINERS

AVAILABLE AT LEADING GARAGES THROUGHOUT THE COUNTRY

---

without doubt

you can rely on

MINTEX
BRAKE LINERS

MINTEX brake and clutch liners are available from garages and distributors throughout the country.

Mintex Man

Behind The Scenes of 1950's & 60's Motor Racing

A Tribute To Lionel Clegg

**Guy Loveridge
&
Bob Richardson**

Douglas Loveridge Publications

First Published in 2001
in a
Limited Edition of 1000
of which this is number:

0989

by

Douglas Loveridge Publications
Moss View
85 Warburton
Emley
Yorkshire
HD8 9QP

©Guy Loveridge 2001

Original photographs from the Lionel Clegg Collection
supplied by the Bob Richardson Motoring Library
Edited, annotated and administered by Guy Loveridge

ISBN 1-900113-01-5

Printed and bound in Slovenia
for and on behalf of
Richard Netherwood Limited
539 Manchester Road, Linthwaite HD7 5QX

Forward

    I am delighted to write the remembrance words for this Lionel Clegg book. I knew Lionel well as a friendly, helpful chap who assisted me several times when preparing my rally cars for tough events. I knew Lionel to help all competitors, even if they did not use his Mintex brakes. When I drove with Aston Martin's, Austin Healey, Jowett and other British companies I was always pleased to see and work with Lionel Clegg. We traveled to the Austin Healey team base for the 1953 Le Mans race together in Lionel's Jaguar. He drove so well and fast I joked that he should maybe be driving rather than me! We went then through France with John Wyer and his wife and Reg Parnell of the Aston Martin team, who I also knew well.

    Lionel was a good friend, colleague and supplier. I thank Guy for writing this book and commend it in memory of my friend Lionel Clegg who assisted me often, even when my rally car was not fitted with his brand of brake and clutch linings. Enjoy the book.

    With best wishes,

        "Gatso."
        Maurice Gatsonides.
        Overeen Holland.
        July 1997.

Authors Dedications

IF I HAVE ACHIEVED any authority as a road transport historian it is due to the help and encouragement of many people over many years. To name them all would be a book in itself. I'm sure they know who they are and how grateful I am. Three people stand out and it is impossible to value my debt to them.

They are:

My Father, whose knowledge I can never hope to equal. From my earliest recollections he always pointed me in the right direction.

Tony Dunning who showed an inquiring youth the workings of his 1903 De Dion. It was he that sparked my initial interest and subsequent collection of motoring books and other memorabilia. I shall always be grateful to Tony for the help and generosity he showed.

Last, but by no means least, Lionel Clegg (always referred to as Mr. Clegg). Time with him gleaned more information than any literature I have read to date. His knowledge, humility and unfailing patience had a profound effect on me. These factors all led to my realizing the struggle that lay ahead for someone like myself wishing to become a credible transport historian. His passing in 1984 brought a sudden realization of the void his death would leave.

Dedicated to Sheila whoses faith in me restored my flaging enthusiasm and gave me something to look forward to.

Bob Richardson.

THIS BOOK IS DEDICATED TO MIKE HAWTHORN. Friend of Lionel Clegg and Britain's First World Champion Racing Driver. It is also dedicated to Lionel Clegg and his memory. My thanks go to Richard Netherwood for his perseverance and friendship and to my friends in the VSCC and the historic motor racing world. You know who you are and, mine's a pint, not 'alf!

Extra special thanks to Roy Salvadori, Sir Stirling Moss, Rob Walker, Tony Brooks, John Cooper, Louis Klemantski, Maurice Gatsonides, Louise Collins, Graham Gauld and Chris Nixon. 'Bless yous' to Victoria, Mum, Dad, Ma and cheers to Richard Burns and Douglas Loveridge, my grandfather.

And most of all to my late Aunt, Christine Clarke, without whose bequest this book would never have seen the light of day.

Guy Loveridge.

J.M. "Mike" Hawthorn 1929 – 1959.

Contents

Testing Times   9

British Grand Prix   23

Le Mans   41

Company Cars   97

So, who was Lionel Clegg?   105
    includes Mr. Clegg – One of Nature's Gentlemen by Bob Richardson

In the thick of it! Mintex at the 1953 Le Mans.

Introduction

ALL OF THE MEN pictured in the photographs you will see in this book are heroes. They raced cars in the era of narrow tyres; drum brakes; cork helmets and cotton overalls. To the paying public of the era, and the readers of 'Motor Sport' and 'Autosport' they were most certainly of another pantheon. To Lionel Clegg, they were clients and friends. Lionel lived his career within the inner circle of world motor racing. His daily activities were concerned with Jaguar, Lister, Lotus, Connaught and Aston Martin. His friends and drinking partners were Mike Hawthorn, Peter Collins, John Wyer, Reg Parnell and Duncan Hamilton.

Lionel travelled across Europe in order to look after the interests of 'his' firms and their drivers; to ensure that their brakes and clutches were operating to their optimum and that, if he could help in any way, he was there to do so. As has become clear, Lionel was more than ready to assist anyone in the motor racing world who might have needed his help. He operated at the Mintex test grounds at Sherbourne in Elmet, where he watched Duncan Hamilton and 'Wilkie' Wilkinson coax nearly 200 mph out of the Ecurie Ecosse D-types. At Silverstone, where Reg Parnell was pleased to 'act the goat' for Lionel's camera during an Aston Martin test session and at the greatest race in the world, Le Mans. His slightly 'illegal' but highly amusing role in a certain Yorkshire car manufacturers' success at La Sarthe will be illuminated later in this book!

I will be eternally grateful to Lionel for having had the foresight and imagination to take a camera and colour film with him on his assignments. His legacy is contained within these pages. That he loved his job is without doubt, that he was supremely good at it is evidenced by the success of the teams he looked after. The high regard with which he was held has been clear in the discussions and correspondence I have had with people who knew and worked with him.

Bob Richardson was chosen by Lionel to be the custodian of the photographs and stories contained in this book. I am grateful for his friendship and encouragement through the seven years this book has taken to compile. I hope that I have done Lionel and his memory adequate service.

Guy Loveridge
Emley,
West Yorkshire,
Spring 2001.

Mintex Man

Testing Times

MINTEX WERE FORTUNATE ENOUGH to have their own dedicated testing track at the former WWII bomber airfield at Sherburn in Elmet near Leeds. So as well as attending team tests and races, and using the industries' own facility at M.I.R.A., Lionel (pictured below with the proving ground manager, Ben Mawson) was able to test brake materials "at home". On one occasion the Ecurie Ecosse team came on their way to Le Mans. "Wilkie" Wilkinson was working on the fine-tuning of one of the D-Type Jaguars they were due to run. The driver blasted off along the runway and returned a quarter of an hour later, complaining about lack of power. "Wilkie" looked at Lionel, winked, and went over to the driver. "What revs were you pulling?" he asked. The answer given, "Wilkie" pulled out his slide rule and began great calculations. "Well then" he said after a few minutes. "With this gearing, is 198 mph not enough for you then?" Because of the flat nature of Sherburn, with no reference points near to the track, the driver had been blissfully unaware of his shattering performance!

Lionel's work with the Mintex Test Fleet involved many punishing miles on the roads of the West Riding. Here he pushes a Standard Vanguard through a ford near Elland. The Vanguard, although a popular family saloon, was also a successful competition mount on events like the Monte and RAC Rallies.

Mintex Man

The freshly fettled Aston DB3S works cars are wheeled out of their transporters at Silverstone on 16th July 1953. Here Reg Parnell's DB3S/4 stands in front of Peter Collins' half unloaded 3S/2. Peter was on the Alpine Rally with Sunbeams and so missed the first day of practice at Silverstone. The cars look superb and show no traces of the mauling they received only a few weeks before at Le Mans.

Mintex Man

Along with the other specialist firms of the 1950s, Mintex prided themselves on offering a fast and efficient competitions department service to their clients whenever they were competing. Here the Mintex Van is at Silverstone with the Aston Martin DB3Ss for the 100 mile sports car race which preceded the 1953 British Grand Prix. Lionel's colleague, Bob Aston, oversees the work of two Mintex technicians.

Mintex Man

Reg Parnell, one of Lionel's closest friends in racing, clowns for the camera at Silverstone. Reg was successful as a driver, both pre and post war and stayed on at Aston's as competitions manager. At the outbreak of World War Two, Reg bought-up a number of "obsolete" racing cars and stored them for the duration, selling them on at the end of the War, at no small personal profit!

Reg Parnell and Roy Salvadori wait for practice to start at Silverstone in 1953. Between them these drivers would amass over thirty years of frontline competition race driving. Reg was actually banned from driving at Brooklands for his part in the huge accident which befell popular female driver, Kay Petre and retirement only came to him in the mid '50s. Roy started racing straight after World War Two and his achievements included the first British Grand Prix at Silverstone, works drives in Formula One, victory for Astons at Le Mans in 1959 and ultimately being part of the development team for the all conquering Ford GT40.

Mintex Man

During bad weather at Silverstone in the 1950s the only place to shelter was the pit garage. Here, John Wyer's wife Tottie, is distracted from her job on the stop watches by team drivers, Salvadori, Collins and Parnell, mechanic Bryan Clayton and Mintex man Bob Aston. Has Lionel just cracked a joke, or do they know of the success to come?

The Aston Martin pits at Le Mans. Note the hessian covered fuel filler nozzle and the different coloured drinking flasks: each driver wanting a different drink during his stint in the car. The ladies are wives, girl friends and secretaries of the various Aston personnel. The factory that races together stays together perhaps?

Mintex Man

17

John Wyer, the Aston Team Manager, oversees a plug change on Roy Salvadori's DB3S at Silverstone in July 1953. Fred Shatlock being entrusted with the work. He must have done his job well as Roy finished 2nd in an Aston clean sweep!

Mintex Man

After the debacle at Le Mans in 1953 the Aston works were determined to make amends in the 100 mile sports car race at Silverstone, a support for the British Grand Prix. Careful testing found that a different back axle ratio from that used at Le Mans would be required and so Park Gear Works in Huddersfield managed to turn out a pair of 3.91/1 clusters almost overnight for the Parnell and Collins cars. Here Roy Parnell watches Aston mechanics Jack Sopp, Brian Clayton and John King looking over one of the team cars. Avon 'red spots' were used by the team as they were of a slightly softer compound. Again, repeated testing showed that, despite fears to the contrary, these tyres would last the full race distance at Silverstone.

Mintex Man

19

Reg Parnell and Peter Collins listen intently to the good counsel of a race official at Silverstone in July 1953. If Peter looks tired, he has a right to be as he had only just returned from an ill-fated Alpine Rally as a member of the Works Sunbeam team. His pairing with Ronnie Adams was, perhaps, not one of Norman Garrard's best decisions. Stirling Moss and Mike Hawthorn, also in the Sunbeam team, both achieved Alpine Cups.

Reg Parnell moves out of the Silverstone pits in Roy Salvadori's DB3S/3. Note the great interest in what was, still, a new car. This was only the Aston's 5th event and much was expected after victories at the British Empire Trophy on the Isle of Man and at Charterhall. Amongst those trying to get a closer look are David Murray (in yellow cap), Wilkie Wilkinson (further white overalls) and Ninian Sanderson of the Ecurie Ecosse and David Macdonald (Dunlop Mac) and Vic Barlow, competitions representative of Dunlop, interested, no doubt, in the performance of the special Avon 'red spots'. Reg is sharing Roy's car as the work required on his car after Le Mans had not been completed in time for this, the first day of practice.

Mintex Man

Above: The inside of a Mintex Test Car. Highly modified with temperature and humidity gauges, decelerometers and wheel revolution counters. Lionel always had much to concentrate on. All Mintex liners had to withstand 100 stops from 50 mph without fading.

Left: The specially adapted Mintex Leyland bus, used to test both brake and clutch facings literally to destruction. It could be ballasted with weights to simulate any loading or vehicle configuration. The hills around Hebden Bridge provided ample gradients for full range testing.

Mintex Man

British Grand Prix

LIONEL'S YEAR WAS NEVER COMPLETE WITHOUT the annual working visit to the British Grand Prix. During his tenure with the Mintex Competitions Department the race was held at Silverstone, Aintree and Brands Hatch, with Silverstone being Lionel's favourite. Lionel witnessed some stirring races and valiant drives but, being a Yorkshireman and Englishman, he was most proud of Stirling Moss and Tony Brook's all British win at Aintree in 1957 and Peter Collins and Mike Hawthorns' superb 1-2 for Ferrari in 1958. Lionel took great pride in 'his' companies success, but nothing could eclipse the joy he felt at seeing his friends beating all comers.

Mintex Man

Stirling Moss. One time 'Boy Wonder' of British Motor Sport and, in later years, "Mr. Motor Racing". Now, in his 71st year and a Knight of the Realm for his services to Motor Sport. This pictures him at the 1953 British Grand Prix meeting where he would race in 2 events; piloting a Cooper Norton in the Formula III race and a Cooper Alta in the Grand Prix itself. He won the 500cc event from pole position and came no-where in the Grand Prix with the Cooper Alta Special. Note that Stirling, ever the professional, wears his laurel wreath surrounded monogram to the left breast of his overalls.

Mintex Man

A picture of great significance. Ginger Devlin stands with arms folded beside Eric Brandon's Francis Beart prepared and entered "double knocker" Cooper Norton. Checking the tyre pressures is "Dunlop Mac" – the world famous David MacDonald, habitué of Brooklands and adviser, friend and confidant of the great "Speed Kings". Like Lionel, "Dunlop Mac" was a familiar figure at race meetings of this era. In the 15 lap 500 cc race Brandon, an ex Cooper works driver and boyhood friend of John Cooper would come home in second some 16 seconds behind Moss, to winnings of £35:00!

Ken Wharton, one of the un-sung heroes of British motor sport. Ken was a true all-rounder and came up through sporting trials and hill climbs, claiming National titles in both disciplines. He ran at Le Mans three times and tamed the V-16 B.R.M. Here he leans over his works Cooper Bristol at the 1953 race, which he would bring home as second British car in eighth place. His death while racing was both sudden and, obviously, tragic. Sadly, little is now remembered of this Smethwick garage owner whose best memorial is surely his four back-to-back British Hill Climb Championships.

Mintex Man

George Abecassis leans on the back of his works HWM Jaguar in the paddock at Silverstone on the 18th July 1953. Behind him Duncan Hamilton signs autographs and chats to adoring fans, looking flushed with success having won Le Mans in the XK120C Jaguar, scarcely one month earlier. Abecassis, along with John Heath, was the driving force behind the HWM (Hersham and Walton Motors) which from 1948 to 1956 was a privately owned and run racing team giving Grand Prix debuts to drivers such as Moss, Collins and Macklin. HWM closed following Heath's tragic death in the Mille Miglia. Abecassis married David Brown's daughter, Angela, and often campaigned works Astons. Sadly Angela died during the proof reading of this book.

"Drunken" Duncan Hamilton, Le Mans winner, war time Fleet Air arm pilot and general 'bon viveur', has a nose through some of Lionel's slides during practice for the 1953 race.

Mintex Man

Duncan Hamilton at the controls of his works entered H.W.M during practice for the 1953 event. Having shared the winning Jaguar XK120C with Tony Rolt at Le Mans the previous month, Duncan's confidence was high and he was enjoying his racing life to the full. In the Grand Prix he started from the 5th row of the grid, 2nd fastest of the H.W.M.s but a full four seconds slower than the slowest of the Ferraris. Some consolation then, perhaps, that he and Tony were feted with a lap of honour in the Le Mans winning Jaguar during the lunch break.

The Formula II Connaught owned by Rob Walker. This was surely the most reliable of racing cars: it finished in the top three 28 times, including 16 wins. This was its only mechanical failure of the season, Tony having overshot his pit during the race and stripped a half shaft key in selecting reverse before the car had come to a halt. This was replaced after the race by a mechanic's screwdriver blade and in that form Walker himself won the racing car class at Ramsgate Speed Trials the next day! No wonder Rob still owns the car. Rob Walker himself is on the right of the picture, in the mackintosh, happily chatting to some schoolboys.

Mintex Man

Tony Rolt, pre war E.R.A. driver of notable success, wartime Major and prisoner of Colditz Castle, was Rob Walker's driver in the 1953 event. Here he sits in gardening gloves and a heavy sweater. Rolt's car was one of five Connaughts entered for the race, this being the period when Grand Prix racing was held under the Formula II rules and thus British cars stood a better chance of competing with the Continentals.

Mintex Man

Dr Guiseppe Farina, perhaps the greatest link between the pre-war 'aces' and the World Championship Drivers of the 1950's. Not a medical doctor, but a thinking driver and member of the works Alfa Romeo team by 1937, winning the last pre-war Grand Prix for them in 1940 at Tripoli in the 158. Post war, he moved back to the Alfa Romeo team and carried on almost where he left off, winning the inaugural World Championship in 1950. His last Grand Prix win came in 1951 and he retired in 1956. Sadly and senselessly he was killed in a Lotus Cortina on an icy Alpine road in 1966. Denis Jenkinson said of him "He was not the best driver of his era, when he won his title, but he was competitive at all times". His 'brio' was such that even Stirling Moss modeled his relaxed driving style upon that of the good Dr Farina.

Mintex Man

33

Alberto Ascari, rated by Mike Hawthorn as greater even than Fangio, walks from his car after practice. Here at the peak of his of his career, Ascari's loss of the French Grand Prix, to team junior Hawthorn, had ended a run of 9 straight wins. He won here and went on to give Ferrari their second World Championship in succession. Sadly, this would prove to be the penultimate win of his career. Notice John Cooper walking from the Ferrari, cleaning his hands, over Ascari's right shoulder. Taking notes for the next Cooper Bristol, perhaps? John encouraged and supported the research for this book. It is very sad that he was never to see a complete copy, dying on Christmas Eve 2000.

Ascari checks on his collar as his great friend and mentor, 'Gigi' Villoresi packs his bag on the pit counter. Behind them, in the beret, is Parenti, a mechanic with Ferrari since the original "Scuderia" days with Alfa Romeo. 'Gigi' also raced for Ferrari pre-war. Ascari, a most careful and superstitious man, would end his life in a borrowed sports car testing at Monza, less than two years after this photograph was taken. He had survived a ducking in the harbour at Monaco when his Lancia D 50 span through the waterside barriers, but then threw his usual caution to the wind and tested in borrowed helmet……..his test lasted about three laps.

Mintex Man

Froilan Gonzales contemplates his works entered Maserati. Along with team mates Fangio, Bonetto and Marimon, the Maserati entry was highly fancied to reverse the result of the previous World Championship event at Reims where Mike Hawthorn beat Fangio by a second after two and three quarter hours. It was not to be, however, as this time it was Ascari who led Fangio home by a minute. Gonzales hung on to take 4th place, one down on his third in France.

Mintex Man

Gonzales, showing why his nickname was "The Pampas Bull", chats with team mechanics before practice for the 1953 event.

Mintex Man

The Maestro about to go to work. No one's list of the top five Grand Prix drivers of all time is complete without Juan Manuel Fangio. He dominated the World Championship for eight years, from its inception to his retirement. All of the other drivers respected and admired him, a measure of this coming in the 1958 French Grand Prix. Fangio had entered in an obsolete Maserati 250 F, and was running in a distant fourth. Mike Hawthorn, wining going away, came up behind "The Old Man", but backed off to avoid the great Champion having the ignominy of being lapped in his last race. Fangio never forgot that gesture. Here in 1954, however, it is a very different story. Mercedes Benz are back in full time racing and Fangio has won the first three races of the season (albeit two of them in a Maserati) and all expected a Silverstone repeat. Unfortunately the all-enveloping bodies on the cars were useless at Silverstone and thus this is a very rare photograph, not least because it shows an undented car! Unable to see the wheels and correctly place the car in the corners, all of the Mercedes Benz team bent their mounts. At the flag Gonzales romped to only his second win, Mike Hawthorn coming home second in a Ferrari 1-2. Fangio struggled to a lowly (by his standards) forth. Fangio only lost twice in 1954, here at Silverstone and in Spain where it was Hawthorn's turn to win for the Scuderia.

Mintex Man

Louis Rosier, French Champion, winner of many non-Championship Grand Prix and, in 1950, winner of Le Mans in a Talbot-Lago 1-2. Rosier is, perhaps, the least well known of the "Big Three" French drivers of the period. Maurice Trintignant, a Monagasque, and Jean Behra are well remembered but Rosier is little honoured today. He raced, rallied and maintained a garage business, all quietly and with great charm. Here he campaigned his own Ferraris in both the Grand Prix and the Formula Libre event. In the 1950 Le Mans race Rosier drove for all but about 20 minutes, only trusting his son for the time it took him to use the lavatory, eat a banana and drink a mug of coffee.....

Mintex Man

……..Rosier's mount in the Formula Libre race was the exact same car Gonzales used to win at Silverstone in 1951, giving Ferrari their first Grand Prix victory! After over 100 events, and many placings, Louis finally lost the race at Monthlery in a Ferrari sports car during the Coupe de Salon. He had the misfortune to linger for a few weeks after his smash. Duncan Hamilton, who witnessed the crash and went on to win, was moved to re-evaluate his own racing career and said in his autobiography "Touch Wood": "As I stood by his grave….I wondered whether the thrill and excitement of the race was worth while when it so often ended like this."

Mintex Man

Le Mans

LE MANS WAS THE HIGHLIGHT OF THE SPORT CAR YEAR. Lionel took the opportunity of the race to spend a week abroad with friends and colleagues, and to entertain the other representatives in the Mintex Pit. (See below). A classic tale of Lionel's involvement with Le Mans centres upon the Jowett team in 1951. Trying to repeat their Class win of the previous year, Jowett's had entered three cars. Lionel paid a visit to the Yorkshire firm's pit during the first hour of the race to find a distraught Horace Grimley, their competitions manager. Apparently the wrong carburettor jets had been fitted and the cars were using too much fuel and not getting high enough speeds. Lionel, knowing that the cars could only be serviced with spares and tools carried on them from the start, suggested an outlandish solution to Horace who, by now desperate and willing to try anything, agreed.

Each time a works car spluttered into the pits Lionel waited for the appropriate moment; stepped forward, coughed into his hand and extended it to shake the driver's. On each occasion the driver's initial look of complete bewilderment was immediately replaced by a broad grin, an extra shake of the hand and then a rapid fixing of the car: re-setting the carbs with the suddenly discovered correct jets! Jowett's went on to achieve their class win. Lionel had, of course, concealed the jets in his cheek and was passing them into his hand for each driver's use. Rules are for the abeyance of fools and the guidance of wise men……

They're off! The famous Le Mans start. Interesting things to note are the chap running the wrong way (!) and the Peerless works car, number 24, in its only Le Mans race. The car ran very well on its Triumph T.R. 3 1991cc engine, to come home in 16th place, having averaged over 83 miles per hour and achieving a third place in the 2 litre class. This car is now fully restored and living in Cumbria and was taken back to Le Mans for some celebratory laps in the 1990's.

Mintex Man

43

David Murray – the driving force behind Ecurie Ecosse. One time racing driver and accountant himself, David's dream was to have a National racing team for Scotland. Through C-type Jaguars, a Cooper-Bristol and the legendary D-types he achieved his ambition. Here he stands on the pit counter in 1957, a thoughtful look on his face, wondering if they can put another one over on Ferrari, Astons and Porsche? Of course, the answer was yes and it was Jaguar number 3 that did the job. Of the first six cars home this year, five were Jaguar D-types. The blonde gentelman in the stripped Bretton shirt is Sir John Whitmore. Later to be British Saloon Car Champion and Lotus Cortina and Mini ace.

Mintex Man

'Wilkie' Wilkinson, partner and chief mechanic with Ecurie Ecosse. 'Wilkie' was already a distinguished and accomplished mechanic pre-war, with the Evans Family at their Belle View garage and then Billy Cotton the bandleader and amateur racing driver. He is best remembered, however, for his efforts with the deep blue cars from Merchiston Mews, Edinburgh – The Ecurie Ecosse. Here he poses by one of the 1957 Le Mans cars. Victory would be theirs again and the small, fan club backed team would once more have humbled the Sports Car world. To think that Jaguar had abandoned racing in 1956 because 'Lofty' England did not think that the D-type could be made to win again!

Mintex Man

45

The winners! Delivering the last of Jaguar's Le Mans victories until the 1980's, Ron Flockhart drives the victor past the pits on the way to their well-deserved prize giving. Ivor Bueb is perched on the near side rear wing, enjoying his second taste of Sarthe victory. 'Wilkie' Wilkinson is walking alongside the car's left hand side, almost guiding his charge safely back home again. This D type was the ex-works 3.4 litre carburettor car, as damaged in practice for the 1956 race by Desmond Titterington. It was crashed very badly by Ron Flockhart in Buenos Aries at the beginning of 1957 and rebuilt by the Jaguar factory in 3.8 Petrol Injection form with a 2.69:1 rear axle ratio. Subsequently the car took part in the "Monzanapolis" Race-of-Two-Worlds, and has been seen more recently in the capable hands of auctioneer and B.R.D.C. member, Robert Brooks.

The second placed Ecurie Ecosse D-type Jaguar, driven by Ninian Sanderson and Jock Lawrence, passes the pits on its way back from a victory lap. David Murray, unable to get even close to the winning car, has hitched a lift on the bonnet of one of "his" cars. What a performance by a small team – previously regarded as an oddity, run as a personal fiefdom and treated as a gentleman's club. Superb!

Mintex Man

47

Fourth place for Paul Frere and "Freddy" Rouselle in the Ecurie National Belge D-type Jaguar was a superb reward in 1957. With works support they rounded off a Jaguar 1 to 4. This car, XKD 573, was repeating exactly its result from 1956, when Rouselle shared with Jacques Swaters. The car led an interesting life, including being used on the road for work commuting in Belgium in the 1960's. It returned to the U.K. in the 1980's, after racing at Suzuka's opening event in Japan. (It came in 8th.) It is still in its Belgian yellow today, owned by John Coombs and campaigned in historic races by such drivers as Martin Brundle. Note that Lionel has tried to get shots of all of the finishers in front of the Mintex advertising banner, canny or what!

More from 1957. Duncan Hamilton, after falling out with 'Lofty' England over team orders at Reims (Duncan decided that he was going to win, rather than back off and obey orders) had flirted with a Ferrari works drive. But then bought his own D-type and invited American sports car ace (and alleged heroin addict) Masten Gregory to co-drive with him. Gregory was no stranger to big engined sports cars, having been a private entrant of Ferraris for many years. He would go on to race Lister-Jaguars with Ecurie Ecosse who were, of course, second time winners of the 'Vingt Quatre Heures' this year. The Hamilton team came home a strong sixth.

Mintex Man

"Ivor the Driver". Ivor Bueb, one of the stalwarts of the Formula III movement where he drove both Arnotts and Coopers; a grand prix racer for Connaught and, perhaps at his best, D-type driver supreme. He sprang to international prominence in 1955 as Mike Hawthorn's 'stand in' co-driver in the winning car. In 1956 they teamed up again to come home a valiant 6th after fuel injection problems delayed them. The injected D-type was still good enough to set a lap record in Mike's hands, however. Here Ivor is back in a Jaguar for 1957 and his third of five runs in the event. He will win again, sharing an Ecurie Ecosse car with Ron Flockhart. A calm garage owner from Cheltenham it was Ivor who appeared with Michael Aspel on the B.B.C. news coverage of Mike Hawthorn's death on the Guildford by-pass. Ivor himself lost his life needlessly after a Formula III race in France. He was taken to hospital following a huge crash, and was left with no one who spoke any English. Drugged and in pain he only had a ruptured spleen. An easy operation even then but, sadly, Ivor died. He was only 36.

1953 and Jaguar are back with three team XK120Cs and a works supported car to make amends for the debacle of 1952 when, as defending winners, the cars had been hastily re-designed, in the hope of finding higher top speeds on the Mulsanne straight. Sadly, all they achieved was inadequate cooling and retirements, despite some last minute 'hammer work' on the bonnets by team manager 'Lofty' England. Here is the full team, lined up in front of their pits. Nearest the camera is the Peter Whitehead/Ian Stewart car, it would come home in fourth place, after holding a watching brief throughout the race, always ready to move up and take the fight to Ferrari or Alfa Romeo should the faster cars pull out. Also notice the personnel here, on the counter is Stirling Moss, squatting to talk to his team manager, 'Lofty' England. In the pits Sir William Lyons can be seen, and around are drivers Stewart and Whitehead. All four of these works "lightweight" cars are still with us. XKC047 (the Belgian entry) is in California; XKC051 (the Rolt/Hamilton winner) lives with Duncan's son, Adrian in Hampshire. It has been re-bodied, although Adrian still owns the original 'clothes'. He found a mummified orange in the car when he had the body replicated, a sure sign of its provenance as Duncan always had an orange with him on long distance sports car drives! XKC052 (Ian Stewart and Peter Whitehead) was last heard of in Exeter; XKC053 (Stirling Moss and Peter Walker) now lives and is raced in America by Terry Larson. Pride was certainly on the line this year, but 1st, 2nd, 4th and 9th made an emphatic point: the Big Cats were back!

Mintex Man

51

The Sergeant-Lumsden lightweigh E type coming home in 5th place at Le Mans in 1962. This car was later sold to the pair of Peters and was raced extensively at Goodwood, Silverstone, Nurburgring etc. It was re-bodied as a low drag coupe in 1964 and retired from Le Mans that year. The car has recently returned to a former owner, David Cottingham, after many years in the United States.

World Championship Class. 'Dead' cars in the paddock. Here in 1953, at his first Le Mans, Mike Hawthorn was paired with Dr 'Nino' Farina in the 4.1 litre 340 MM Ferrari. Sadly a mistake by the mechanics led to the brakes having to be topped up with fluid before the rules allowed them to be, and this led to the car being excluded from the race. Bizarrely the author saw this car under a dustsheet in Norfolk during the summer of 2000. Note the professional looking Bristol transporters in the background and the French Nash Healey which retired momentarily before the Farina/Hawthorn car.

Mintex Man

The Alfa Romeo works team. The original of this picture was filed by Lionel in amongst his Le Mans pictures, there are three cars here, and with race numbers 23 and 68 discernible, I have been unable to work out what year this is! Still, a good one for 'Classic and Sports Car' magazine's "Hauls of Fame" feature. Anyone who knows the answer please let the author know.

1962 and one of the three Fiat Abarth team cars. Abarth entered seven cars in this year's race under the wings of both Simca and Fiat. The Fiat based variants ran in the experimental category, but the experiment failed with only one Abarth finishing (behind the Morgan!) This car driven by Fraissinet and Condrillier lasted 13 ½ hours only to expire with a blown engine.

Mintex Man

Phil Hill and Olivier Gendebien's Ferrari 330 LM comes back to the pit area at the end of the 1962 race. This win completed a hat trick for Gendebien, and was his forth overall. It was also Phil Hill's third win. They also managed to break Mike Hawthorn's five year old lap record. Ferrari won both the Experimental and G.T. classes this year. Notice the radio reporter with his back-pack sized transmitter by the car's front wing. My, how times have changed!

1961 and the works Ferrari mechanics celebrate a superb 1-2-3 and the GT class win. Here, at about three minutes past four, the mechanics who have been looking after the 250 TRI/61 of works drivers Willy Mairesse and Mike Parkes climb aboard for a lap of honour. Winners in '61 were Olivier Gendebien and Phil Hill, making it three wins for Gendebien and two for the pairing. It was a stiff fight between the official works team and the North American Racing entry, spearheaded by the Rodriguez brothers. Sadly their challenge ended in the 23rd hour whilst pushing hard in second place.

Mintex Man

A broad view of the Healey headquarters for Le Mans 1953. Noteworthy in the picture are the Mintex International Racing Service yellow van; Donald Healey's personal Austin Healey 100 road car, left hand drive, but GB registered with BARC and BRDC badges of both pre and post war vintage. Lionel's own XK120 and the Mintex "crew bus", a battleship gray Standard Vanguard are pulled up at the edges of the courtyard. Also of note, it is all being done in the open air! Might the goose have appeared later on the dinner menu?

The Healey Team at their chateau base in 1953. This year saw the debut of the Austin Healey 100 with the Donald Healey motor company alongside the American liveried Nash Healeys at Le Mans. In 1952 the Nash Healey had come home third behind the two Works Mercedes. Here Maurice Gatsonides, whose idea it was to base the team at the chateau, chats with Geoff Healey whilst the mechanics work on the ill-fated number 10 car of the French pair, Cabantous and Veyron, who would retire after only 1 ½ hours racing.

Mintex Man

Donald Healey chats to the Lady of the Chateau as Geoff enjoys a characteristic cup of tea. He and "Gatso" look on as Maurice's car is prepared. He would finish a creditable twelfth overall, sharing with Johnny Locket.

The full Healey effort lined up for practice at the 1953 race. Despite being painted in American racing colours, the two Nash Healeys are right hand drive and carry 'G.B.' plates. The French pairing confer in their car, entry number 10. They will not, in fact, trouble the timekeepers for long! The other cars, however, run consistently throughout the 24 hours to come home in 11th, 12th and 14th places – a most satisfactory team result.

Mintex Man

Bruce McLaren, works Cooper driver and winner of four Grand Prix from 101 starts, here samples Le Mans for the first time in 1959. He was sharing a Cooper Monaco with Jim Russell, which crashed while in 9th place. Bruce would win at Le Mans in 1966 with fellow Kiwi Chris Amon in the Ford GT40. He seems pleased to see Lionel here, but his experience this time out would sour him to round the clock racing. Russell crashed out at Whitehouse on some oil and suffered extreme burns. From then on Bruce saw the race as a contractual obligation, nothing more. Driving in 1966 was part of the deal for Ford engines for his fledgling Grand Prix team. The win did him no harm, mind you!

Mintex Man

Behind every racing car there is a hive of activity. Here plugs, brakes, clutches and fan belts are fully represented by the good folk of Mintex, Lockheed and K.L.G. all on site and on duty in the 1950's.

Mintex Man

At the back of the Mintex pit stands Rene Thomas(on right) – French motor racing ace; hero of the Resistance; one time land speed record holder; Indianapolis winner; Mintex agent for France and firm friend of Lionel Clegg. Lionel would still vividly recall, years later, how over officious gendarmes would snap to attention and allow Lionel and Rene to pass when they saw his Croix de Guerre and Legion D'honnour medals!

64 Mintex Man

Mintex Man

.........And they band played on. Typical Le Mans scene as a French Scout Band marches past.

Mintex Man

Le Mans 1957. John Wyer, the Aston competitions' manager stands in the pit lane. Behind him is the marker board for the DBR1 shared by Roy Salvadori and Les Leston. This would not be a great year for Astons, with the private car of Colas and Kerguen only managing a finish in 11th place. Also seen here are Roy Parnell, to Wyer's right, cousin of Reg and the Aston test driver. Over Wyer's left arm is Mortimer Morris "Mort" Goodall. Font of Aston Martin knowledge, no mean driver himself and founder of the Aston Martin owner's club in 1935. The rather dapper looking gentleman in the cravat is Aston's P.R. Manager, Alan Dakers. The next 24 hours will test his skills to the full!

Mintex Man

Reg Parnell and Peter Collins at the Aston Martin team's usual Le Mans base, the Hotel de France at La Chartre sur le Loir. It's 1953 and Reg is sorting out something in the boot of a support car and Peter, being interested in all things mechanical, has come to 'have a butchers'. Peter was in the middle of his highly enjoyed time with the team. He would close his association with Aston Martin with a finely crafted 2nd at the 1956 Le Mans sharing with Stirling Moss. Peter had even been employed by Astons in Paris for a time, as a salesman, whilst he honed his racing talents. A good way to avoid national service?

Mintex Man

A study in youthful ambition. This is Jimmy Stewart. As he is wearing a driver's arm band this is most likely to be 1954 when he drove, and crashed, for Aston Martin. Cursed by bad luck, he was unlucky enough to be given one of the aerodynamically appalling DB3S coupes. He had made his name with the Ecurie Ecosse Jaguars, but had been signed up by Aston's to share with Graham Whitehead. Sadly, this race would see Jimmy having a huge accident when the coupe simply 'took off' and put him off the track on the approach to Maison Blanche, all might not have been lost if the Talbot of Meyrat had not then crashed into the wreckage its self. Jimmy escaped with a broken arm., which took a long time to mend, Jimmy's next major race being the Nurburgring 1000 miles in 1955. Back in the bosom of the Jaguar works, he had the misfortune to re-break the same arm having inverted his D-type. He was advised by doctors to retire. A sad end to a highly promising career, but his baby brother, always interested in the sport, managed to make a bit of an impression in the future. His name? Jackie, of course.

Mintex Man

Here in 1953 Reg Parnell warms DB3S/2, which he was to share with Peter Collins, at the pit counter. Aston works mechanic Jack Sopp keeps a careful eye on the clocks whilst Reg gives it the gun and discusses the forthcoming race with Bob Aston, Lionel's colleague from Mintex. Sadly, Reg clouted some trees at Terte Rouge on the 16th lap whilst leading the Aston team in 14th place. The car was too badly damaged to continue and of the three Aston starters, none went all the way. An inauspicious debut for the DB3S outside Great Britain.

Mintex Man

Seeing the funny side! Standing behind one of the team DB3Ss and with Carol Shelby's American liveried car, Reg Parnell seems to be enjoying life at Le Mans in 1954. He would not be quite so cheerful at 1pm on Sunday as his super-charged car blows its head gasket and becomes the fifth and last Aston to retire. Scant consolation came from never having run outside the top ten.

Mintex Man

On the way to Le Mans in 1953, Lionel traveled with Maurice Gatsonides and in convoy with John and Tottie Wyer and Reg Parnell. Here they are parked in the square at Le Mans, by the cathedral. In the background is John Wyer's Aston Martin DB2/4 drop-head and Lionel's Jaguar XK120. The Jag was a 'company car' which was on long-term test, and used in the development of brake linings and clutch facings. Reg is holding up a cloth duster with the 'Mintex Brake Linings' logo on it. Quite an endorsement given Reg's record with racing cars, stretching back to Brooklands and Donnington in the 1930's. During the war Reg gave shed space to probably 75% of the racing cars in Britain during the hostilities.

Mintex Man

1954, and John Wyer and Bob Aston pose for Lionel's camera in the pits on the Saturday morning. Behind them is one of the DB3S coupes which would cause so much trouble and strife for the team during the race. Bob was a very colourful and well loved figure on the international racing scene and would, by the end of the 1950's, be very closely involved with the works Cooper effort, even running the stop watches in the pit for them.

Mintex Man

Roy Parnell and Alan Dakers confer in the Aston Martin pits on the Saturday morning. In contrast to his last picture, Reg does not look particularly confident and, as it would work out, with good reason as only the privately entered DB3S of Colus & Kergen in eleventh place would finish, staying the course ahead of the three DBR1 and 3S works cars. Shape of things to come for 1958?

Roy Parnell and Carroll Shelby share a joke across Carroll's own DB3S in the pits before the start of the 1954 race. The race was a disaster for Aston's and Carroll was not exactly impressed with the performance of his car. Being used to Allards in racing back in the USA, Shelby was expecting huge speeds on the long Mulsanne straight. He could only get up to 140.2 mph over the flying kilometre. This was a good 10 mph down on the Brixton 'hybrids'. Even Peter Collins, the fastest of the Aston DB3S drivers, could only achieve 144.2 mph. The writing was on the wall for Astons as the Ferraris were doing 160+ and the D-Types 172.9!

Mintex Man

Le Mans, 1953. The Aston Martin DB3S/3 of George Abecassis and Roy Salvadori sits in the pits during practice. The car looks ready to go. Note that each of the cars had a different coloured grille; designed to make identification easier, and also note that the cars here have the early 3S style of grille, closely echoing the "portcullis" look of the preceding DB3. Frank Freeley's superb styling is shown off to good effect from this angle. The DB3/S is surely one of the prettiest sports cars of any era. Sadly the performance did not live up to the looks and all three of the team cars entered this year were to drop out. Of particular embarrassment to Lionel and Mintex, this car failed due to a terminal clutch fault after only 9 hours whilst in 41st place. They had been as high as 17th.

Mintex Man

Flying buttresses abound in this picture of the 1953 line up, taken from the pit counter. Of particular interest is the 1100cc OSCA, number 48. This was a special Vignale bodied car, entered in 1952 and 1953 by Damonte. Chris Nixon muses in his excellent "The Aston Martin DB3S Sports Car" whether Frank Freeley 'borrowed' his inspiration for the DB3S wing line from the Italian special the previous year. (Freeley himself, in an interview with Brian Josceleyn, denies any inspiration, claiming to have done the design on his own, allowing the air from the blanking plate between engine and radiator to escape. As he said "If only we had known enough to put an air damn on the front of the DB3S".) Either way, imagine the cars passing through the pit area at night at 120 mph and then take a close look at the top left edge of the picture in front of the cars. That is the earthen banking at the edge of the track. Easy to understand how the 1955 disaster came about.

Mintex Man

Aston works mechanic Brian Clayton waves to attract a friend's attention in the pits before the start of the 1954 Race. Judging by the packed grand stands, this is Saturday morning with only a few minutes to go before the track is cleared. Maybe he has opened a book on how long the cars will last and wants to get some bets on before the start! Although the lines are smooth and sexy, the cars are a disaster and will both come close to killing their drivers during the race.

Mintex Man

Roy Parnell poses in front of the number 20 Aston Martin's pit at the 1954 event. Looking happy and relaxed Roy is pleased to 'mug' for his friend Lionel. Behind him, one of the open team cars is checked over, the headrest being open to allow a 'plombier' access to the fuel filler. Number 20 was one of the closed "Saloon/Coupe" cars, and not an open version.

Mintex Man

1958 and it looks as though something is bothering both Reg Parnell and John Wyer. Maybe the French program has spelt their names incorrectly? They had good reason to look worried, as it turned out, as all three of the works Astons failed to last the course, these all being DBR1's, supposedly the new car to take the championship. Face was saved, however, by the Whitehead brothers' ex-works DB3S which came home a superb 2nd, less than 100 miles behind the works Ferrari of Phil Hill and Olivier Gendebien. The weather was, unlike in this photograph, appalling! Rain fell for most of the race, Graham Whitehead later recalled that the conditions were so bad that "At one stage I did the whole of the Mulsanne straight in third gear, as I couldn't see where I was going!"

1958 again and the private entry DB3S of the Whitehead brothers. Already 5 years old and abandoned as a front line works car by Aston Martin, the car, benefiting from superb preparation and careful driving saved the English firm's blushes by coming home in second place. This same car, DB3S/6 had, numerically, come second at Le Mans before in 1955 as a works car, when driven by Peter Collins and Paul Frere. Quite an achievement considering it had competed in 18 International races in between, being placed no less than 6 times, including 2nd's at Rouen and Aintree! The most successful Aston DB3S of all?

Mintex Man

Ambition satisfied! 1959 and Aston Martin lines up with a team of four DBR1 three litre cars. The best drivers, including Stirling Moss, Roy Salvadori, Carol Shelby, Paul Frere, Maurice Trintignant and Jack Fairman are there along with a works supported DB4 in the G.T. class. After two second places, (Moss and Collins and Collins and Frere) the British team is confident of victory. At the end of the race it is an Aston 1-2, with the Ferraris in third to sixth places inclusive! Salvadori and Shelby have set a new class record and in doing so have traveled over 150 miles further than the 1958 winners. They also handed Astons a superb chance to go on and take the Sports Car World Championship – they did so and David Brown's smile is the widest it has ever been.

The Gerard and Clarke Frazer Nash in the pits before practice for the 1953 event. This Le Mans Replica was a very well campaigned car even then, at only three years old! Bob Gerard, ERA exponent and journeyman racer, having won his class in the Tourist Trophy with the car in both 1950 and 1951. The car is still used today, in the caring ownership of N. Curtis.

Mintex Man

I think that this is one of the prettiest cars ever built. The Vignalle bodied 1100cc O.S.C.A. To be driven in the 1953 race by Damonte and 'Helde'. Damonte had run this car in 1952 with a 1342 cc engine, but had retired in the 19th hour with clutch problems. In 1953 he ran with the 1033cc engine and a change of co-driver. They achieved 18th overall and first in the 1100cc class. If at first you don't succeed.......!

A DB Panhard HBR, driven to 18th place in 1961 by Laureau and Bouharde. This was a most successful year for the DB Panhards. Of the six cars entered, five came home, although admittedly in the last five places, securing the Index of Performance with the tiny 702cc engine in this car. Now, does anyone see echoes of the MG A in this car's design or is it just me?

Mintex Man

The 1958 race and the notorious Sarthe weather has claimed another two victims during the night. The Lotus XV, with its 1476 cc Coventry Climax engine has been misfiring, no doubt as a result of the deluge getting to the electrics. The driver, Jay Chamberlain, loses concentration momentarily as he approaches the Dunlop bridge, spins and strikes the bank. Jay manages to climb clear, but suffers concussion and is led away to recover. It's indicative of the seriousness of the Saturday night's conditions that at just past 11:30pm the private Ferrari 250 TR entered by Francoise Picard missed the inadequate warnings of the Lotus's wreckage and hit the British car, causing extensive damage to the car from Maranello. Luckily Picard also escaped with only minor injuries. He had been lying 10th at the end of the previous hour, the Lotus in 37th. Trouble amongst the journeyman racers.

Francoise Pascalle's Ferrari TR 250, chassis number 0748, after it's massive night time accident. A typically French Gendarme regards the wreckage. How much would that car be worth today? £2.5 million? Probably.

Mintex Man

Lotus Elevens. Lotus entered four cars in the 1957 race and all four finished. The best placed being the farthest from the camera here, the 1097 CC Climax engined car of McKay Fraser and Chamberlain. In travelling 2377.982 miles at an average of 99.088 miles per hour they set a Class G record (751-1100cc). In the next class down the middle car here, number 55, running the 745cc Climax, Allison and Hall also set a new record. This time taking it from the DB Panhard with an increase of over 230 miles distance and nearly 10 miles per hour overall. The 41 car nearest the camera came in 16th overall. This was without doubt Lotus' best year at Le Mans.

Mintex Man

The Triumph TR4'S'. These cars used an experimental twin cam version of the venerable four cylinder engine, first seen in the 1940's. The three car team all ran well and came home in 9th, 11th and 15th. Here the Les Leston and Rob Slotemaker car is readied for practice. The driver in the canary yellow overalls, incidentally, is Peter Bolton. He and Ballisat led the team home. Peter is an extremely accomplished racing driver, often seen in AC Aces and, in a few years time from this photograph, to be one of the first drivers to race the Cobra at Le Mans. ....

Mintex Man

....these cars were, incidentally, the reason that Morgan were refused a run at the 1961 Le Mans. Standard-Triumph had far too much money in the 'Sabrina' engine to risk it being beaten by a normal 1991cc T.R. engine, as fitted to the Malvern product. So, words were had behind the scenes and the Morgan was not allowed to run for being "old fashioned"! All things being equal, on its 1962 performance the Morgan would have come home in 12th place, splitting the T.R. team. Ends justifying means, anyone? (Rob Slotemaker would drive works Morgans at Spa and the Nurburgring in 1963, winning class awards, and would go on to contest the London to Sydney rally in 1970.)

Mintex Man

1959 and the works Lotus Elite sits in the pits. Jim Clarke and Sir John Whitmore are the drivers. The Elite was a superb competition machine, two of them finishing in the top 10 this year. This was the year of a classic bit of 'kidology' by Colin Chapman. As previously noted, only spares and tools carried in the car could be used during the race. When the heat of the engine cooked the car's starter motor and it refused to work, all was thought lost until Chapman ordered a bucket of water to be brought to the pit. When the car next came in, much was made of removing the jammed starter and exclaiming abour the heat . The mechanic dropped it in the bucket, from where a satisfying cloud of steam arose. He then removed the starter and re-fitted it. Hey presto the motor worked and the car roared back into the race! The French judge of fact, with tears of laughter in his eyes, commended Chapman on his cheek and said nothing further. (Of course he had a spare in the bucket!)

Mintex Man

It is 1961 and Peters Harper and Proctor take the Index of Thermal Efficiency in their Sunbeam Alpine Harrington Le Mans coupe. Running in the G.T. class this product of a Hove based coach builder has beaten Lotus, Panhard, Porsche, Abarth and Ferrari in the coveted Index; a typically French and confusing measure of "ton-miles per gallon weight". In layman's terms, they achieved an average speed of 91 miles per hour and a fuel consumption of over 17 miles per gallon. This car only returned to competition in 2000 at the Goodwood Circuit revival meeting, being driven by Clive Harrington, son of the company's founder.

1962 and here we have the 'old fashioned' Morgan entry, sitting in its pit ready for the off. In fact, the car had been thoroughly changed between 1961 when it was turned down at scrutineering and 1962, gaining the first of the 'low line' bodies, and a British Racing Green paint job. Chris Lawrence sits in a deck chair on the pit counter in a Panama hat, looking completely unconcerned. This was a 'low key' works entry by Morgans. In the next pit is the works Sunbeam Alpine, driven by the 'Peter's' Harper and Jopp. This car came home in 15th place, 2 spots behind the Morgan. Lawrence and Shepherd-Barron, in the Morgan, won the two litre G.T. class this year, averaging nearly 94 miles per hour and travelling 2255 miles. Both of these cars are still with us, although there have been a few Morgans which have worn the famous number TOK 258, including one of the ultra fast S.L.R. cars. This car was, in effect, the prototype of the Super Sports model of +4 from Morgan.

Mintex Man

It's all over for another year. It is four minutes past four pm on Sunday afternoon and after the excitement of the previous twenty four hours: the blood, the sweat, the tears and the passion, all will fall silent again for another year. A school boy cranes to see who has come second, but most people are only interested in the winners at the centre of the crowd.

Mintex Man

The hussle and bussle of the Le Mans paddock. Lionel's working week would be mainly taken up with shuttling back and forth between here and the pits. For the Mintex team, the actual race was often only the mid-point of their involvement, as all brake and clutch failures from the race would have to be thoroughly investigated. 'Racing improves the breed' as they say.

Mintex Man

1953 and Lionel has joined colleagues in the Girling pit to watch the start of the race. As ever the pits were crowded and, as Bill Boddy Editor of "Motor Sport"(far right) noted "It was standing room only!"

Company Cars

Lionel's favourite company car. Pictured shortly after he took delivery in April 1955, Lionel's Austin Healey 100 S was a very rare beast indeed with only 50 odd of these cars being produced. Being the holder of many international speed records it came complete with all round disc brakes; a 130 b.h.p. engine; four speed gear box and an all aluminum body. Lionel was in good company as an 'original' 100 S owner, joining Briggs Cunningham, Da Silva Ramos, Raymond Flower and Ron Flockhart. Lionel's car was the 23rd off the production line, immediately after Flockhart's. The 'Mintex' 100 S still exists today, even though it was sold on by the company, and enjoyed a racing career with Dick Protheroe and others. Gerry Marshall drove this car to a fine 2nd place in the Fordwater Trophy at the 2000 Goodwood Revival Meeting.

Mintex Man

Lionel's wife, Nora Clegg.(seen here in the passenger seat). Although she was never the enthusiast Lionel was, Nora knew how to drive and welcomed the 'perks' of a position like her husband's. Here she poses outside their home in Lionel's brand new Healey 100 S. She looks as pleased with it as Lionel undoubtedly was. This vehicle, chassis number 3704 was only the forth 100 S to be sold in England, the rest going abroad. It is now owned by Robert Waterhouse.

Mintex Man

Above: Lionel's 4th company car during his time with the competitions department of Mintex, and his 2nd Jaguar. This distinctively registered XK150 fixed head coupe came with an engine tuned to D type specification by his old friend at Ecurie Ecosse, "Wilkie" Wilkinson. Pace, Grace, Space indeed.

Left: What a contrast to the above, although still a sought after vehicle today. Lionel's first Mintex company car, and the test 'hack' was this 3 litre Bentley. Lionel joined the Bentley Driver's Club and attened at least one of their hill climbs in it. He always remembered this car with great affection.

Mintex Man

Mrs Dick Jefferies. A colleague and close friend of Lionel's was Dick Jefferies of Dunlop. Here she stands in front of Dick's Mk I Jaguar saloon. This car, as were Lionel's 120 and 150, was "breathed upon" by the works. In this case a higher differential ratio, D-type head and sand-cast carburettors allowed for relaxed high speed touring across Europe and just look at the badges:- A.A., R.A.C., B.A.R.C., B.R.S.C.C., B.R.D.C. are just some of those on display. That badge bar would be worth over £1,000:00 today. (If the B.R.D.C. let you sell it!) Not to even mention that registration number!

Mintex Man

The experimental Rover gas turbine car. Another potential market for Mintex clutches and brakes? Maybe Lionel was looking to the future – after all we were all going to be driving these things by the year 2000 weren't we? This car led to the Rover – B.R.M. collecting a large cheque from the Automobile Club De L'Ouest in 1963 when Graham Hill and Ritchie Ginther screamed round for 24 hours, coming home well placed but un-classified as they were running as '00' and not actually competing.

Mintex Man

Export - Import. On the dockside at Dunkirk, Renault Dauphins and Citroën Amis await trans-shipment. A clear indication of the balance between standard and luxury models is provided by the singleton red Caravell at the end of the Dauphin line-up. Pale blue must have been that season's colour.

Mintex Man

Perks of the job. Lionel's private Triumph Herald, purchased on very favourable terms directly from Standard Triumph themselves. Lionel took great pride in his road cars and always enjoyed them to the full. This picture was taken in late autumn sunshine in 1961 just outside Huddersfield

Mrs Clegg's very own day to day transport. A two door Austin A35 in the nearest Lionel could get to British Racing Green. With characteristic "tweaking" by Lionel and his friends in motorsport, this car was reckoned to be capable of a genuine "ton".

Mintex Man

So, who was Lionel Clegg?

Mintex Man

Mr. Clegg – One of Nature's Gentlemen.

LIONEL WHITELEY CLEGG WAS BORN ON JUNE 2ND, around the turn-of-the- 20th Century, to a local textile family; which in Huddersfield at that time was like being nobility. They lived at Grove House, Dalton. At that time quite a rural area. In fact the Great Yorkshire show would be held there in later years. The only reminder of this today is a pub called The Grove.

The Cleggs were staunchly Methodist and attended Queen Street Chapel (then the largest chapel in the world). Today this is the Lawrence Batley Theatre. Lionel remembered their coachman being on call all day Sunday to take the family to chapel as and when required. A fact which, in later years, Lionel was not at all happy about.

Lionel's earliest memories of cars revolved around the family Renault which had been re-bodied by Ripon brothers with 'Roi de Belge' coachwork. That probably accounted for the silver pincushion styled on a Renault he had as a toy which now has pride of place among my model collection.

I know very little about his childhood or his friends apart, that is, from his closest pal, one ER Hall of Aston Martin, MG, Bentley and Le Mans fame. I remember Lionel gleefully telling the story of Eddie trying to parachute from the coach house roof with an umbrella! This resulted in a badly broken leg.

It is ironic that Eddie Hall, who drove at the highest level for many years, only had a bone-crunching accident with an umbrella. Legend had it he used to have to handbrake his cars into his home, Hartley Cottages in Kirkburton!

Motor cycle football in Huddersfield's Greenhead Park in the late 1930's. The crowd at this match was six deep all around the pitch! A potentially lethal sport, no fixture ever ending without the "meat wagon" making a hand-full of visits to the pitch! It was even played internationally, with Troyes hosting a tri-nation tournament in 1932.

In a similar vein it is ironic that Lionel, who competed in dirt track (speedway), motorcycle rodeos (moto-cross), motorcycle football and drove fast cars should himself break a leg when skiing down the slope behind Fartown Rugby league ground in Huddersfield! If Lionel had lived we were to have met Baby Hall, Eddie Hall's Cousin, so that I could discover more about one of England's most private motor racers.

I know nothing of Lionel's early schooldays, no doubt considering his background he would have been to some small, select prep school. The kind with which, at that time, Huddersfield abounded. Later in life he attended Galloway's which I believe was some kind of commercial set-up. By the time he left school the family mill business had been disposed of and he turned his back on textiles to become an apprentice at W C Holmes, a local engineering firm. Even at this early age his love of all things mechanical was beginning to show through. W C Holmes would train many of the sons of Huddersfield's well to do families.

Mintex Man

Whilst there he sought 'light relief' by becoming a bus conductor on Huddersfield transport during the General strike. I still have in my collection a menu signed by all the 'black legs' and some of the signatures make fascinating reading. Many of the people going on to become pillars of Huddersfield society! My mother, now in her late Eighties, still recalls going to "Dead Waters" to watch strikers throw stones at the black legs. Despite troubled times Lionel found time to marry Miss Nora Shaw of St John's Place, Birkby. Lionel recalled teaching his young bride to drive a small Swift motor car. They moved to Halifax Old Road where they remained for the rest of their lives. For a long period he found himself out of work and did occasional jobs for a boilermaker in Thornton Lodge. He laughed as he told me of hiding deep inside the boilers if anybody from the 'social' appeared!

In his motor sporting life, Lionel had won a gold medal in the 'Isle of Skye' (Holmfirth, West Riding) speed hill climb riding a Sparkbrook at a speed of 31 m.p.h. In complete contrast to this achievement was his result at the 'Doncaster Petrol St. Leger' where, on a 125 c.c. machine, he came within 0.1 mph of the world record. Also competing, and winning, that day was George Brough.

Whilst a member of Kirkburton Motor Cycle Club he competed in motorcycle rodeos. In one event at Victoria (near Holmfirth) he managed to finish in second place on his little Francis Barnett to Martin Mitchell's 'Big Port' AJS. As Mitchell later said, "He could certainly make the little bugger go!" I still have the spoon Lionel received for coming second, and the names of the match-winners.

One of Lionel's motorcycling friends sits covertously upon Lionel's own Douglas. A useful machine for off-road use in motorcyle rodeos and scrambles, note the "Universal" rear tyre on this multi-purpose Duggie.

From 1926-1933 Kirkburton Motor Cycle Club was the top club in Yorkshire and had amongst its members the likes of Norman Gledhill, Manx GP winner and Eva Asquith, the lady speedway rider.

Many years ago in conversation with Arnold Moore another of Huddersfield's most famous motor cyclists, I mentioned Lionel. He told me that Lionel used to turn up at his workshop and say: " Mr. Moore, are we going to ride the muddy lanes today?" A few years later he was to be grateful to Arnold, when, on being offered a job testing for Mintex at Cleckheaton, Lionel was able to borrow a motorcycle from Arnold enabling him to get to work.

The position he obtained in the Spen Valley was the turning point in his life. He was now getting paid for doing what he loved. The main part of his job seems to have been long-distance road testing of friction parts using Mintex's three-litre Bentley. He often went over Home Moss, the scene of some of E R Hall's early successes with an Aston Martin. On some of these journeys he was accompanied by R S (Jack) Moorhouse a former Kirkburton club-mate and himself a Manx GP replica winner and a member of K.M.C.C.'s Winning team at the 1931 Manx. Jack himself gave me plenty of time and vouched for Lionel's skill at the wheel.

When war broke out Lionel tried to join the RAF, but was deemed to be in a reserved occupation and was ordered to stay at Mintex to use the knowledge he had gained as his career had progressed. He never went into detail about his war service but I know that he worked on new materials for aircraft disc-brake pads, which Mintex manufactured.

I remember one delightful tale that he loved to tell regarding the development of jet engines. He and some work colleagues were in a pub one night in Gloucestershire when they were approached by a rather genteel elderly lady whose husband had flown with the Royal Flying Corps. She demanded to know why an aeroplane she had seen take off had no propeller. Apparently no amount of flannel would convince the lady that Frank Whittle's finest did not need a propeller! Somehow we manage to keep the Gloucester Whittle a secret. Amazing!

Taken in 1932, Lionel sits proudly in his G.N. cycle car. Registered EH 3775, Lionel rebuilt the car totally, from the ground upwards, documenting his work in a series of detailed photographs. No wonder he is grinning!

On the subject of the Royal Flying Corps, one of its greatest historians was Peter Ustinov, one of our finest actors and himself also a lifelong car enthusiast. Apparently, somewhere on his travels Lionel bumped into the great thespian and, as both were keen fly fishermen, some kind of competition was planned. I believe that all went in Lionel's favour prompting Peter Ustinov to comment that Lionel was "A surprising little bugger". Any stories Lionel told of these meetings with famous people never had the slightest hint of name-dropping. The great got the same treatment as 'his boys' from work.

Despite the pressure of disc brake development Mintex took time out to fit a new cone clutch to Oliver Langton's 1904 Rolls Royce, the oldest Rolls Royce in the world. Lionel, having had a test drive in this car was not overly impressed! Langton was world famous as a Scott works rider and in his later years built up a fine collection of vintage motorcycles.

One of Lionel's trips abroad to took him to Germany where Mercedes-Benz were having great difficulty with the mix of their brake shoes. He discovered the materials were too soft and on sorting them out was taken to lunch in a Mercedes Benz 300 SL Gull-wing driven by Rudolf Uhlenhaut who had lived in Leeds as a student and spoke English with a broad Yorkshire accent! This impressed Lionel more than Uhlenhaut's undoubted skill as a development engineer for all Mercedes competition cars, or as a driver of the same calibre as Fangio and Moss!

In later years Mintex played host to some Japanese and the story goes that while Lionel was explaining some technicalities to his guests he drew a rough graph to put his point over. When he was sure they understood the solution he screwed up the bit of paper and threw it into a wastepaper basket. He then showed his guests round the complex. When the visit was over one of the Japanese approached him bearing the same piece of paper, obviously retrieved when Lionel was not looking. He castigated the offender, mentioning his size, colour and parentage! This kind of

Mintex Man

bad manners where anathema to a man of his standing. For the remainder of his working life he was involved with the development of the disc brake and its teething problems of boiling fluids and warping discs. He visited MIRA, Silverstone and Le Mans and travelled all over England visiting car manufacturers. He spoke kindly of Donald Healey and his products, and seemed quite at ease with the likes of Sir William Lyons, Lofty England and John Wyer.

Lionel made many friends in the Great British car industry of the time and was certainly involved at a great time in the motoring history. He talked of going round Brooklands with Lagonda's Stuart Tresillian, and passed on to me a beautiful Lagonda lapel badge. He was at Donnington to see Mercedes Benz and Auto-Union fight it out and drove Ecurrie Ecosse D-type Jaguars. Many people have written autobiographies without living half the experiences of Lionel Clegg. Yet, as was his wont, he modestly played it all down.

One of Mintex's biggest achievements was the opening of its own test track at Sherburn-in-Elmet. Lionel was involved as much as anyone. This saved the trips to MIRA and gave them an advantage in brake development which they were to keep for many years. It would be unfair when discussing Lionel and Mintex not to mention his great friend and colleague in the Mintex Competitions Department, Bob Aston. He also played a principal part in the Spen Valley firm's achievements at Le Mans, and later went on to become a key part in Cooper's first World Championship. A man Lionel respected enormously. After a lifetime at Mintex, and having seen England as power in both sports and racing cars his last times were spent in a management capacity. He had made way for new blood. He is well remembered for his fairness, understanding and most of all for his empathy. On his retirement he and his wife led a peaceful existence travelling and visiting the many friends made over the years. He carried on his hobbies of fishing and photography, but never lost his love of cars and motorcycles.

Lionel and a colleague, John Fenton had become interested in vintage motorcycles and had competed in vintage trials. Lionel's success relied upon his experience and "low down cunning".

I first meet Mr. Clegg at The Shepherd's Arms public house in Huddersfield. One of the locals who knew of my interest in classic motorcycles pointed out a small, dapper gentleman at the Bar saying, "He's got a Scott". I approached him and, during our subsequent

Above: Taken from the July 18th 1952 edition of "Autosport". Trade representatives, and the title for this book.

Below: Lionel guides his AJS through a Vintage Motor Cycle Club trial near Leeds in the early 1960's. (From the next picture in this series I can tell you he is about to fall off!)

discussion, I discovered he had owned various vintage motorcycles, having previously taken part in vintage trials. Unfortunately by then he had already given them all away. I was later to find how typical this was of his generosity. At this point I had no idea what a phenomenal motoring knowledge he had. Some locals also mentioned that he occasionally arrived at "The Shepherd's" in a selection of Sports Cars.

Our initial conversations were always brief and gave no insight into his exploits on both 2 and 4 wheels. This is something he took for granted and never mentioned unless pressed. Our meetings would probably have remained brief had it not been for one particular incident:-

One day I arrive at the pub with a newly acquired model E-type Jaguar. Seeing this model being displayed to my friends, Mr. Clegg asked if he could also view it. Having done so he told me that he had collected similar models himself. This all lead to his suggesting that we arrange for a date so that I might see them back at his cottage.

Gradually I came to spend more time with Mr. Clegg, always under the ever-critical eye of Mrs Nora Clegg. Being from local nobility i.e. a mill owner's daughter (Shaw's Larchfield Mills) she viewed lesser mortals such as car enthusiasts with miss-guided disdain. Later on when Mr. Clegg was in hospital recovering from a slight stroke I did some odd jobs for her and found out that her knowledge of local textile industry history, especially who-married-who, equalled the motoring knowledge of her husband. I will always regret not writing down for future reference some of her potentially slanderous comments on some of her contemporaries! She was a great character who often pointed out the pretence of money. We will never see her like again. To her textiles was the only trade of any consequence and people like the Browns etc were upstarts not be taken seriously.

An aerial diversion. Lionel was delighted to get involved with the Bristol Brabazon airliner project. This eight engined leviathan of the air had only four air screws and so required complex gearing and clutches to provide the drive. Sadly the Brabazon was already out-dated by the time of its maiden flight from Filton and would soon be broken up and forgotten. Lionel was lucky to get this photograph on one of its few sorties into the ether. Mintex also worked closely with David Brown's who provided a unique towing tractor with ultra low gearing to tow the Brabazon about.

Lionel and Nora Clegg were like chalk and cheese but they enjoyed a long and happy marriage although sadly, they were never blessed with children. After Mrs Clegg's sudden death my visits to the cottage became more regular. Every Thursday evening at 7:30pm my Morris Minor would be parked outside. On entry I would have a chair, and would see two cans of Stones put on small antique tables and then the quickest and most satisfying three hours of my week would begin. Once we had settled down and made sure each was in good health the discussion would begin. All I needed to do was throw a name at him: car, place or person and he would start to retell his experiences. He had total recall and his stories could be complementary or scathing, and yet causing no offence.

I sometimes think that even if these meetings had gone on forever then his anecdotes and memories would not have been repeated. His comments on racing drivers of the Forties and Fifties were particularly enlightening, and any driver or mechanic not worthy of Mr. Clegg's respect was invariably referred to as a 'spoofer'! One of his favourites was Duncan Hamilton, to whom he always referred as 'Drunken' Duncan, I wonder why?

He also liked to tell stories about his small contributions to the successes certain motor racing teams had. The friendship between our hero

Mintex Man

and Horace Grimley of Jowetts endured throughout Jowetts sporting efforts, and Mr. Clegg loved to tell how he and Horace took the '*pregnant earwig*' (R1 Jupiter prototype) to MIRA in a removal van! On the subject of MIRA, quite a few of Mr. Clegg's stories revolved around the famous test track. One concerned circulating at 70 mph in a Midland red bus; another when he lapped a Connaught faster than a certain World Champion motor cyclist (no-names no pack drill)!

Lionel was also capable of telling lots against himself. Jaguar were one of the first teams to adopt disc brakes and Mintex were heavily involved. One year at Le Mans Mr. Clegg was taking Sir John Fenton for a fast lap in an X K Jaguar when, after breaking sharply at Mulsanne, he warped a disc, and a Knight of the realm was not impressed! His chauffeur was suitably chastised. I cannot imagine anyone doing this to Lionel as someone once said at Mintex that getting a bollocking from Mr. Clegg was a marvellous experience and not to be missed!

Another story he liked to tell was when returning from one of his many visits to Coventry he got stuck in snow driving his Sunbeam Talbot between Glossop and Woodhead. He managed to struggle back to Glossop and spent a night in the police cells as a guest of the Derbyshire Constabulary. A strange venue for a man who had all the attributes of a model citizen! Being a good citizen did not, however, prevent him from getting caught for speeding in Browns Lane, Coventry. In his defence he questioned the accuracy of the police car's speedometer! To a keen motorist that's like getting nicked down the Mall!

Some of his memories were not so light hearted. His account of the 1955 Le Mans crash included information not given to the public until Mark Kahn's book 'Death Race Le Mans' was published. Despite the traumatic experience of seeing the crash from the pits he was able to comfort

Lionel was entrusted with the prototype XK 120 Jaguar in 1948, and he took it to an early race meeting at Goodwood. It caused quite a stir, on its trade plates and being left hand drive clearly destined for the export market.
Note the Austin A90 Atlantic in the back ground. It's failure to capture the American market being in stark contrast to the XK range's success. Still, the failure of the A90 did lead directly to the Austin-Healey range of cars.

the mother of one of our best drivers. He explained to her why, prior to Mercedes-Benz withdrawing, the leading team still continued to circulate at undiminished speed.

Even though Lionel nearly always had a long term test car from Mintex, he had to provide transport for Nora, who herself was no mean driver. I don't know every private car they had, but I do remember that they always seemed to favour small cars of character. Their first new car, after the war, was a Standard Flying Nine tourer, which was soon followed by a grey Singer Roadster. This soon earned its self a firm place in Lionel's affections. This was a three speed model, but when Singer fitted a four speed gear box Lionel immediately had his converted. A nice story regarding the Singer occurred on Lionel's last birthday. A good friend of mine, Ashley Crossland, the motoring author, arrived at Lionel's house in his own roadster and took a very surprised Mr. Clegg out for a spin. To say Ashley made Lionel's day would be an understatement!

After his retirement the Cleggs favoured upmarket B.M.C. 1300's, Riley Kestrels, Vanden Plas Princesses etc. following on from the much loved A35 of earlier years. Later, after his stroke, Lionel bought an automatic Renault 5 and this was the last car in which we travelled together. His skill was undiminished and he took great delight in demonstrating the kick-down! Shortly before his death he bought a Mini automatic, but sadly

Mintex Man

this had little use and eventually, after his death, it passed to one of his friends a few doors down from the house. Mr. Clegg never lost his empathy with all things mechanical and his cars were always maintained to the highest standards.

I have often wondered what a man who drove 'D' type Jaguars, Rover's 'Jet 1' and a Grand Prix Connaught would make of the 21st Century's motor cars?

The nature of Lionel's work meant he had to be driven in cars by some of the leading Grand prix drivers of the time. His comments on some do not bear repeating, only Raymond Sommer escaped his scathing judgements. When one sees the photographs in this book it is obvious the respect Lionel was shown by people in the sport by their body language: they all seem pleased to pose, especially the notoriously reticent Reg Parnell. It is also obvious that Lionel had a soft spot for Aston's, after all both he and David Brown were Huddersfield locals.

Lionel must have met every person involved in motor racing at this glorious time. Some impressed, some did not. One who certainly did, but not necessarily for his undoubted prowess on the track, was B.Bira. Lionel recalled him having a conversation in four languages simultaneously, sounds like the 2000 world champion!

In a world full of wild characters and extroverts, Lionel seemed totally out of place. He was well liked, polite and modest. His skill behind the wheel of a sports car, however, left no one in doubt about his bravery. These were the days of seat-of-the-pants driving remember and some of the cars of the Fifties, when taken to the limit, could be very unforgiving.

Although he was surrounded by great and powerful people, he had a huge respect for his Mintex team and always referred to them as 'his boys'. Later, at his funeral, I was to meet the same men and I can assure you that the respect was mutual. As one of the team said, to drive a car into fog at well in excess of 120 miles an hour takes a lot of skill and bravery!

Lionel's closest friend in the trade appears to have been be Dick Jefferies, his opposite number at Dunlop. Lionel was even godfather to Dick's daughter.

Over the years I knew Lionel he generously gave me many bits and pieces he had collected. Badges, models and trade freebies. The silver car which he had as a boy and a Ecurrie Ecosse cigarette case presented to him by David Murray in recognition of his assistance to the team. This remains my most treasured possession.

Left: Lionel's first toy, a pin cushion in the form of a veteran Renault. Lovingly cared for, both by Lionel and Bob.

Right: Another prized possession. Lionel's gold Ecurie Ecosse cigarette case. A personal gift from David Murray following the team's victory at Le Mans in 1956.

Our meetings on Thursday nights could have gone on forever but for a visit to a concert where Lionel caught a bad cold. He phoned to say he was not fit to see me but, to put my mind at rest, I called unannounced. That he was very ill was obvious so I called on his neighbour, a great bloke called Brian Fawcett who promise to keep an eye on him, as he always had.

I received a phone call from Brian shortly afterwards to say that Lionel was in hospital with pneumonia. On Christmas Day I went with Lionel's lifelong friend Nora Wimpenny (whose father was works manager at Karrier Motors) to see Lionel, and he seemed to be on the mend at last. This was not to be. He was old and frail, and had suffered a kidney failure and his condition deteriorated rapidly. Soon after this, on a very wet evening, I went to hospital to give Nora a lift home. I put my head round the ward door to tell her that I was there. She said "Lionel, Bob's here" and he called me

Mintex Man

113

Lionel's beloved 'Nash. Apparently the ex-works short chassis Nurburg trials car. This machine ran in the Monte and Alpine in 1933 and also competed at Brooklands and in numerous hill climbs. BUT, this is more likely to be 'Mr. Tinker's' car. He went to the works to buy chassis number 2026, and also purchased the chassis number and registration of the, by then, broken up works car. The body was a second hand T.T. Replica's, but not from the original "MV"'s glory days. This car was reported as being "Complete on its wheels" in Holmfirth after the 1939-1945 war. Confused? Imagine how I felt researching all of that! To add to the effect – Lionel has written on the back of the big picture:- "Yeah man! (Rasp!!!) Hi-de-hi!" How's that for motoring history!

to his bedside. Even though he was very weak he still apologised for the trouble he thought he was causing. Truly a gentleman to the very last.

A few weeks before Lionel's illness my Morris 1000 Traveller was written off outside his house by a hit and run driver. Lionel felt responsible and was very upset. The day before his death the police sorted to it out. My last words to Mr. Clegg were to assure him that all was well. He was very relieved. After a few more words he lapsed into unconsciousness and I never spoke to him again. One of the worst experience of my life. The following morning I received a call at work from my wife. One of the most important people in my life was gone.

Even though Lionel got to drive some of the finest sports cars of the day he never lost his love of motorcycles. When I first got to know him he had in his garage a Honda 90. It had covered only 365 miles in seven years. Lionel used it to travel up to Outlane to photograph the construction of the M62. As readers have seen Lionel's knowledge of all things on wheels was equalled by his skills with the camera.

The Honda 90 came into my possession along with a collection of model cars for £25. Incidentally, among the models was Lionel's own favourite racing car: an original Scalextric Ferrari. Having run the Honda for year and not been able to come to terms with Japanese rubber, it was put with the rest of my old motorbike collection in the cellar of a chapel. On the night of Mr. Clegg's death I went and sat on his old bike and thought long and hard about what I had lost.

As I mentioned earlier, at his funeral I got to meet some of 'his boys' and it was a complement to me when one of them said "Bob, you will feel the loss more than anybody".

A timely phone-call from Brian a few days later found me back at the cottage where I found these photographs. They have made this tribute possible. Lionel had always wanted his photographic memories to come to me. He often said that I was the only one to appreciate them. I hope I can do justice to his faith in me. Mr. Clegg never achieved fame like Chapman, Lyons and 'Lofty' England but his contribution to Britain's success on the tracks and the road is no less worthy of note.

If what I have written makes people aware of the stature of this marvellous man I will feel I have repaid a small amount of what he gave to me.

After his death I realised I was one of the very few to have visited him. I hope our meetings relieved some of his loneliness. They certainly made me very, very happy. Mr. Clegg I still miss you.

Year after year
many important events
are won by
drivers
who specify
MINTEX
brake liners

Where high performance counts you can rely on

MINTEX

MINTEX Brake and Clutch liners are manufactured by British Belting and Asbestos Ltd., Cleckheaton, Yorkshire. All MINTEX products, including Automotive Fan Belts, are obtainable from MINTEX Service Depots and Stockists throughout the country. B.B.A. are also the manufacturers of "SCANDURA" the original P.V.C. Fireproof Conveyor Belting.

In any country...
In any event...
you can rely on

MINTEX
BRAKE LINERS

AVAILABLE AT LEADING GARAGES THROUGHOUT THE COUNTRY